Humor
with a **Halo**

Humor
with a Halo

AL FASOL

True Funny Stories
From
Church Life

C.S.S. Publishing Co.
Lima, Ohio

HUMOR WITH A HALO

Fourth Printing 1991

Third Printing 1991

Second Printing 1989

Copyright © 1989 by
The C.S.S. Publishing Company, Inc.
Lima, Ohio

LIBRARY OF CONGRESS
Library of Congress Cataloging-in-Publication Data

Fasol, Al.
  Humor with a halo.

    1. Christian life—Humor.   I. Title.
  BV4517.F37   1989   250'.207   88-24264
  ISBN 1-55673-115-9

9826 / ISBN 1-55673-115-9

To the memory of
Grady Nutt
a man gifted of God
for Christian humor
and
To Dr. Paul Hunsinger
who teaches and lives
in the joy of the Christian life

Table of Contents

Preface

"A time to weep, and a time to laugh;"
(Ecclesiastes 3:4a)

The Bible, it is true, does not contain a great deal of humor. It is also true that the Bible is not devoid of humor. The Bible, despite the presence of judgments, tragedies, and restive "thou shalt nots," is an amazingly pleasant book. The very concept of grace and salvation means to be open, free, spacious, free from danger, free from sin. There can hardly be a more meaningful and exhilarating experience than to become a child of God. In fact, the sense of deliverance and redemption pervades the Book. The word "joy" is often associated with salvation in the Bible. The word joy occurs in Scripture nearly two hundred times, and every reference is related to either a present or a future circumstance. The Lord himself often calmed the disciple's fear by saying, "Be of good cheer . . ." Laughter is mentioned in the Bible nearly twenty times in a positive way. (The other references to laughter are negative, such as laughter of derision and scorn.) Elton Trueblood feels that most of us overlook humor in the Bible, especially in the teachings of Jesus: "We do not know with certainty how much humor there is in Christ's teaching, but we can be sure there is far more than is normally recognized."[1]

The first mention of laughter in the Bible is a hearty one. Abraham literally fell upon his face laughing at the prospect of Sarah bearing him a child at their advanced age. (Genesis 17:17) Sarah joined in the merriment. (Genesis 18:12) Their fun was short-lived as they realized that, indeed, nothing is too difficult for the Lord. Significantly, Abraham and Sarah's child was named Isaac which means "He laughs."

[1]Elton Trueblood, *The Humor of Christ*. New York: Harper & Row, 1964. p. 10.

What a simple yet complicated thing laughter is! Too often laughter occurs at someone else's expense. Is it appropriate to laugh when someone else is serious, as was the case with Abraham and Sarah? Is it appropriate to laugh when someone else is hurting, as with the sons of Sceva in Acts 17? Is it appropriate to laugh with scorn, as in Psalm 2:4? The answers depend on the people involved and the kind of situation in which they are involved. Abraham and Sarah laughed because they thought parenthood at their age *sounded* hilarious. The sons of Sceva were laughable because of the ridiculous position in which they had put themselves. God laughed with scorn at the self-importance of those who thought they could take his place. (Psalm 2:4) The problem is, when laughter has to be justified, the urge to laugh is lost.

One of the most unfair things I have ever heard about laughter is that Christians rarely laugh. For many persons the stereotype of a Christian is that of a stoic, non-smiling person living in the confines of a multitude of "thou shalt nots." Such a stereotype may be true of some Christians, and even some sects within Christianity. Christians in general, however, have more fun than anyone in the world. This collection of true humorous anecdotes of the Christian life is representative of the ways in which Christians enjoy themselves. Laughter is a hallmark of the Christian life. This book is not an anthology of Christian humor. Such anthologies have been written and are available at various book stores. This book was written so that everyone can *enjoy the joy of being a Christian.* Christians will read these anecdotes and find many people they know. I hope that the non-Christians who read this book will want to know more about the exciting and joyous experience of becoming a Christian.

All of these anecdotes are true stories. Those who shared them with me had to swear that they were eye and ear witnesses. I have discarded enough stories to write a book of equal size because they were not verifiable. I have also discarded numerous stories that seemed to be indelicate and would, perhaps, be unnecessarily offensive to someone (the spirit of Romans 14:1-12 is reflected here, I hope).

Names of persons and places were deleted so as not to embarrass anyone. Where names are used, they are used with permission of the persons involved, and are used only because they were necessary to the story, or because the persons involved preferred that their name be used.

This short book was written with assistance from Mrs. Barbara Walker, Mrs. Barbara Kent, Mrs. Nancy Owen, and Mrs. Dian Kidd. Responsibility for content is mine, of course.

Even though the Bible does not contain many direct references to humor or laughter, and even though the Bible is devoid of "jokes," the Bible is an immensely cheerful book and gives rise to the Christian life which is the most pleasant, joyful, happy life possible.

Chapter One

■■■■■■

The Delightful Humor of Children

Most of the time, children are delightful people. They are often unabashed, almost always straightforward, lots of fun, and entirely unpredictable. The beauty and joy of children was expressed on several occasions by Jesus: "Suffer the little children to come unto me . . ." ". . . become as little children . . ." ". . . He took a child, and set him in the midst of them: and when he had taken him in his arms, he said unto them, 'Whosoever shall receive one of such children in my name receives me . . .' " The innocence of little children was captured in two sentences in a Ben Hayden sermon: "What will heaven be like? It will be like little children." Almost annually at seminary graduation services, a new graduate will be pleasantly embarrassed when a child's voice calls out from the audience, "That's my Mommy!" or "That's my Daddy!" It is the one interruption that is universally tolerated and, perhaps, universally coveted.

Anyone who has not been pleasantly surprised, made speechless, and/or driven to gales of laughter by the antics of a child has missed too much of life. Everyone who has ever marvelled at the joys of being Mommy or Daddy, or grandma or grandpa, or teacher or friend of a little child will find someone they know in these true, humorous stories of children in the context of the Christian life. For example, you might recognize this nine year old boy who taught his young pastor:

A Lesson on Pride

The young pastor was enjoying his first pastorate. When he arrived the year previous at that little church in Royalton, Illinois, an attendance level of thirty would have been considered outstanding. On this Sunday night before Christmas, however, the church was packed! More than 100 people had found a place to sit in the pews, and at least twenty others were looking for a seat. The pastor delegated four men to drive to the funeral home to request the loan of some folding chairs.

The one room church was abuzz with the sounds of fellowship. A curtain had been drawn across the platform and the children were behind it excitedly getting into their costumes for a Christmas play.

The pastor had just announced that this special Sunday evening service would be starting a little late so that everyone could be seated for the Christmas play. The pastor then moved to his left and stood in a corner between the platform and the congregation. In the back of his mind he was thinking of how he would tell the ministerial alliance meeting that he had to stand throughout the evening service because there was not one seat available for him.

In the front of his mind, the pastor was marvelling to himself: "When was the last time, if ever, that this room was filled to capacity? Had anyone from the church or any church in this town ever had to borrow folding chairs from the funeral home? Is it not a good thing I happened along when I did to get this church on fire?" The situation was ripe for the dangers of pride and the preacher was indulging himself fully.

As the pastor stood there, hands behind his back, rocking a little on his feet to vent some of the excitement he felt, nine-year-old Danny D. came out from behind the curtain and stood by the pastor. Denny, too, put his hands behind his back and rocked on his feet. This was not entirely unusual. Denny's father had not been attending church and the pastor was one of only two young men to whom Denny could relate in the church. After a minute or so the conversation between Denny and the pastor was opened by Denny.

"Quite a crowd tonight, huh pastor?"

"That's right, Denny," said the pastor, brimming with self congratulations, all of which were decimated when Denny asked:

"Preacher, have you ever noticed that we have our largest crowds when you're not scheduled to preach?"

"Out of the Mouths of Babes . . ."

The revival was to have a new twist. The pastor of a church near Atlanta, Georgia, noticed that most of the young couples in the church would attend only the Sunday morning service. The reasons offered for this generally centered on the children. "We don't want to keep the children up too late," people would argue. The pastor suspected these "reasons" were really excuses. He had visited many of these families when the children were up well past the 8:00 end of evening service time. He had also seen these families at several community functions with their children, that ended well after 9:00 p.m.

The pastor used the ancient church strategy of scheduling children to participate in the revival worship services. Their participation was to be an active one. He was not going to bribe them with candy bars or gold stars on an attendance chart. Nor was he going to offer just a "children's sermon" and then dismiss them to another part of the building for refreshments and games. No, he was going to give the children a priority time in the worship service. He visited Sunday church school classes and enlisted six prodigious six-year-olds to read a verse from the Bible and to say whatever they wished to say about it.

The guest preacher warned against having this recital immediately before the sermon. The preacher rightly complained, "They are a hard act to follow." The preacher was proven correct in the first service. The first reading and comment from

Scripture was by a girl. You can imagine how primly and properly she was dressed in lace and ruffles for this special occasion. She marched smartly to the microphone, took a deep breath and in one sentence said, "Honor-thy-father-and-thy-mother-that-thy-days-may-be-long-in-the-Lord-sometimes-I-do-sometimes-I-don't-amen!"

* * *

For reasons known only to little girls, she resented the fact that she was born third of three children. Her resentment was such that on her third birthday she announced that she was really five years old. And so she was "five years old" for three years. Presumably, being five years old in her mind meant she was catching up to her older brother and sister.

One day when she was three years old (or, one day when she was in her first of three years of being five years old) she rather purposefully brought a family album to her mother. "Show me the pictures," she commanded. There were pictures of Mommy and Daddy, brother and sister, and a few other relatives and friends. Then the purpose for this viewing session emerged.

"Why aren't I in this picture?" demanded the little girl.

"You weren't born, yet." said the mother smiling.

"What does that mean, 'I wasn't born yet'? "

Predictably, mother was a little bit at a loss for words, but gave what she hoped would be sufficient explanation for a three-year-old. It wasn't nearly enough information for this girl.

"Then why wasn't I in this picture?"

"Because," said mother with a little less of a smile, "you weren't born yet."

"If I wasn't born yet, then where was I?"

Before mother could think of an answer to that one, she asked again, "Why aren't I in this picture? I see Mommy and Daddy and brother and sister, but I don't see me. Why? and don't tell me I wasn't born yet!"

Mommy, barely restraining herself from shouting, answered, "But that's the answer to your question! You just had not been born yet!"

"Well, where was I if I wasn't born yet?" screamed the daughter.

"You were in heaven!" shouted the mother.

The little girl pondered for a while, calmly took the picture album and put it away. On the way back to her room, she stopped and glared at her mother and said, "Well, I'm sure not there now!"

* * *

Romance blossoms early for all of us, if we are lucky. At the end of Sunday church school a preschool girl came out to her parents with a delicate smile and a friendly wave to a dark-haired boy. "What did you learn in Sunday school?" asked the parents. "I learned that he likes me," said the little girl, rather resignedly. "You learned that Jesus likes you?" asked the parents. "No," answered the girl with some exasperation, "I learned that Lance likes me." "Oh," said the parents, somewhat bemused, "and how do you *know* Lance likes you?" "Because," said the girl in the midst of a stifled giggle, "he spit on my table."

* * *

The guest preacher was invited to have Sunday lunch at the home of a young couple in Lawton, Oklahoma. The couple seemed a little tense. The preacher soon realized the pastor had drafted them for this responsibility in the misdirected hope that the experience would make the young couple more faithful in their attendance.

The preacher was invited to ride with the family. The preacher climbed into the back seat with the couple's four-year-old son. The two "men" in the back seat immediately struck a friendship, much to the relief of the couple who felt they had no idea how to talk to a preacher. The conversation in the back seat was animated. The little boy, as if prompted by the parents, asked the preacher if he liked ham. "Oh, yes," said the preacher, to the relief of the parents. "And, how about you," asked the preacher, "do you like ham?"

"Yes!" said the boy. "Preacher, would you slice my ham for me?"

"Sure! How many slices would you like?"

"Oh, about a hunnert!"

And so the conversation went.

When lunch was prepared, and they sat around the table, the boy started reaching for the mashed potatoes. The mother gently disciplined the boy. The boy was confused. Why were they at the table, except to eat? As the adults bowed their heads to say grace (an irregular experience at the boy's house), he suddenly caught on. Just as his father inhaled in preparation to say, "Our heavenly Father" or something to that effect, desperately wanting to impress the preacher, the boy shouted, "Hey, Dad!"

"What is it?" asked the father, barely concealing his irritation.

"Could I be the one that talks to the plate this time?"

* * *

The daddy had made a basic mistake. He realized it too late. How could he ever make it up to his little girl? It was a Saturday afternoon. As was his custom as a good daddy, he took his son and two daughters with him in order to spend some "quality" time with them. It was a blustery March day — perfect for kite flying. There were lots of kites in the air when they arrived at the park. Dad, of course, had some trouble getting the kite up. Every kid there had a kite up, but not Dad. There was at least a partial explanation for this. Dad noticed a gang of bullies tormenting some of the children and he was concerned about his son and older daughter, who had their kites up on the other side of the park where the gang was circulating.

When he finally got the kite up, the younger daughter, by his side, was exhilarated. Dad, however, was preoccupied with his other two children.

"Daddy, may I hold the kite?"

"Sure. Hold on to the string real tight."

The girl was utterly fascinated and thoroughly proud of herself.

"I'm a *big* girl now, aren't I, Daddy? . . . . Daddy? Daddy, are you listening to me?"

"What? Oh, of course, I was watching your brother and sister, but, yes, you will always be my *little* girl, that's right."

"No, Dad. That was wrong." In a huff, the little girl punched her father's leg, and handed the kite string back to him. As she stomped away toward her brother and sister, she shouted over her shoulder, "Hummph, and you will always be my *fat* Daddy!"

* * *

Maybe it was because it was a *university* Baptist Church. Perhaps, children at a *university* church are supposed to be precocious. The Sunday church school teacher in the two-year-olds department heard a squabble over a puzzle. Seizing the initiative, she decided this would be a good time to teach a lesson.

"Ben," Miss Beverly said, "you should share the puzzle."

"Why should I share the puzzle?" asked Ben who had reached the "why" stage and probably every other stage earlier than he was supposed to.

Miss Beverly thought her answer would surely pacify a two-year-old: "Because the Bible said we must share."

Ben thought only briefly about this before he went to Miss

Beverly's personal belongings, found her Bible, took it to Miss Beverly and demanded, "Show me where it says in the Bible that I should share my puzzle."

* * *

The baptismal service is a quiet ritual at many churches. On this occasion the lights were dim except in the baptistry. The pastor's son was impressed to see his father in a white robe — impressed, but not speechless. Shortly after immersing a young woman, the pastor heard his son shout, "Ooh, Daddy, you're in trouble. You got Tommy's mommy all wet!"

* * *

The pastor took his son on a hospital visit. He soon realized it was a mistake. This Roman Catholic hospital had rules against little children visiting in the rooms. The pastor told the boy to sit in the lobby while he stepped down the hall. The little boy, fascinated by the strange looks, sounds, and smells of a hospital, indicated he would be fine.

A nun in her white nurse's habit came in the lobby and was surprised to hear a little boy say, "I know you. You're Mrs. Santa Claus aren't you?"

* * *

The interim pastor of the First Baptist Church of Seymour, Texas, pulled in to a service station one Saturday night. A white pickup with a camper pulled out, heading west, just as the pastor pulled in. A few seconds later, a five- or six-year-old boy came from the side of the station, hitching up his jeans. The pastor correctly surmised that the little boy was supposed to be in the truck that just left. Rather than approach the boy too quickly, the pastor sat on the concrete step in front of the station office and smiled pleasantly at the boy.

"I know you. You're Mrs. Santa Claus, aren't you?"

The boy looked for the white pickup around the station, next door at a cafe, and glanced up and down the highway. Fighting his panic, the boy squared his shoulders and moved toward the smiling man.

"Say, mister, do you know who I am?"

"As a matter of fact I do. You're the little boy that got left at the service station in Seymour tonight."

Somehow the answer reassured the boy. The pastor advised him to sit down and wait till his parents realized he was gone and could come right back here after him. (The pastor was praying that they would miss him before they got to Lubbock, or even Clovis, New Mexico).

To while away the time, the pastor decided to tell the boy all the Bible stories he could think of. More than an hour and a few dozen Bible stories later, the white pickup finally returned. The boy ran out to it, and as a door on the cab opened, the boy stopped and the pastor heard what an impact the Bible stories had made when the little fellow yelled, "That man over there said God doesn't like for you to go off and leave little boys!"

* * *

Child number eleven and child number twelve were both boys. Number eleven, much like the ten before him, resented the new "baby" of the family. Number eleven went out of his way to torment his brother. He would whack him real hard, and then, as number twelve started to cry, would exclaim, "I'm sorry. I didn't mean it. Don't tell Mom and Dad. Here, let me rub it. It doesn't hurt does it? I'm real sorry. Don't tell Mom and Dad and I promise I won't do it again."

The scene was repeated often. Anyone who has had two or more children will testify to the familiarity of this story.

However, one day number eleven sneaked into position behind number twelve, threw a body block into his brother that sent him sprawling into a rugged drainage ditch beside the road in front of the house. This time with sincere urgency, number eleven apologized profusely: "This time I really *am* sorry — I really mean it. Don't cry, I really am sorry." In wisdom beyond his years, number twelve yelled back at his brother, "I know you're sorry. What I want to know is, when will you be sorry enough to quit?"

* * *

The father wanted to teach Christian principles to his three-year-old son. He was weary, though, of his son coming in whimpering every time another child hit him. Finally, he said, "Son, I can't be there to protect you all the time, and evidently turning the other cheek doesn't apply to little boys, I just don't know. Let's try this. Next time someone hits you, you hit him back."

A few minutes later the father heard another boy cry out and head for home. His son came marching in with a triumphant glow on his face.

"Did you hit him back, Son?"

"No, Daddy, I hit him head!"

* * *

Her daddy was thirty-seven years old when he finally received his Ph.D. She was just four-years-old and not all that impressed. Her mother overheard this conversation with a preschool friend:

"What kind of doctor is your daddy?"

"I don't know."

"Does he help people?"

"No."

"Does he fix teeth?"

"No."

"Does he take care of animals?"

"No."

"Well, what does he do?"
"He's a doctor that doesn't do anything."

*   *   *

The little boy had asked his Sunday church school teachers the same question for several weeks: "Are you mad?" The answer was always a pleasant, "No, Johnny, I am not mad." But Johnny persisted, "Are you mad?" His teachers gave their usual response, but their curiosity was piqued. One teacher decided to respond positively. All of the teachers were tuned in as Johnny asked them, one by one, "Are you mad?" When one teacher responded, "Yes, Johnny, I am mad. I am as mad as I have ever been in my life!" Johnny put a hand on his teacher's arm, and said with a shrug of his shoulders, "Why don't you cheer up?" and was never heard to ask the question again.

*   *   *

It was a matter of deep concern to the little boy. The pastor had come to visit the children's Sunday church school departments. The visit had been anticipated, and the children were encouraged to ask any questions of the pastor.
"Pastor," Tommy asked, "will God provide harp lessons in heaven?"

*   *   *

It was said in all innocence, but it was humorous. The family was on the way to visit their previous pastorate. They recalled the names of old friends and recounted some good times. During a lull in the conversation, one of the children leaned toward the front seat of their station wagon and said, "Dad, those people really love you . . . I wonder why . . .?"

*   *   *

She was sitting on her father's lap. They were having a great conversation, until he said that he was proud of his son and was proud of his little daughter.

"But, Daddy, I don't want to be no little dotter."

"Why? What's so bad about being a daughter?"

"Because, if Robert is your sun, I want to be your star or moon, but I don't want to be no dotter."

* * *

It was a heated discussion, but the adults were outnumbered. The five-year-old girl was adament. She would wear her new red dress or she would not appear in the Christmas pageant. First, the director of the children's play begged her: "Please, put on the costume. The people want to see you in Mary's costume." "No!" replied the girl. "Either I wear this new red dress or I do not go out on that stage!" Next, her Sunday church school teacher pleaded with her: "This costume is just like what Mary would have worn. Mary was the mother of Jesus and you want to be dressed just right for the part, don't you?" "No!" answered the little girl. "Either I wear this new red dress or I do not go out on the stage!" Finally her parents instructed her: "You must wear the costume, because when you are on the stage the people are to think that you are Mary. The people will be confused if you wear your new red dress." "No!" responded the girl. "Either I wear this new red dress or I do not go out on that stage!"

Clearly, the adults were outnumbered. An emergency conference was held. It was already past time for the play to begin. The play director stepped in front of the curtains, greeted the congregation, apologized for the late start, and explained:

"Due to circumstances beyond our control, Mary the mother of Jesus, will appear tonight only in a new red dress."

Immediately afterward, before the director could leave the stage, everyone heard a little girl's voice from behind the stage curtain shout:

"If Mary had had a new red dress, she would have worn it!"

* * *

The decision was finally made. After weeks of visiting churches, father and mother finally decided which church they would join. It was a difficult decision. They had many friends, including the pastors, in the various churches. It was a difficult decision, but it was a relief to have determined where they would place their membership.

They could not join the church of their choice this Sunday, though. They had promised another pastor that they would visit his church this Sunday. However, the Sunday after that they would join the church of their choice.

On the way to the church which they had promised the pastor they would visit, they discussed the matter of church membership. The older of their two sons leaned forward to ask, "Is joining the church when we walk down the aisle and people shake your hand, and the old ladies hug us?" "That's right," assured the father. "And we will be getting that over with soon now."

The little boy, being raised in a Baptist family, naturally took that answer literally. To prove that he was a big boy that needed no coaching or instruction, he dutifully started down the aisle during the invitation hymn at the end of that morning's service.

"Where is he going?" asked the mother.

"To the bathroom, I guess," answered the father.

"Honey, I don't think so," observed the mother. "I think he is heading right for the pastor."

"Oh, no! He thought I meant we were joining this church this morning."

"Honey, hurry and get him before he gets to the pastor!"

Too late. The boy wearing a broad grin, was telling the pastor that his family is joining the church this morning. The father turned, and with a wan smile and shrug of the shoulders waved for his wife and other son to come forward, too. Some day you may meet a Baptist family who will laughingly tell you how they happened to join the wrong church.

* * *

During the quiet, meditative time in which the offering plate was being passed, a little girl melodiously announced, "You're right, Daddy! They *do* take dimes!"

* * *

The pastor asked a public school teacher if his son could ride in her car pool to the child-care center near the school. The teacher obliged. The boy sat in the front seat. On the way to school that morning, a car ran a stop sign, and made a turn going the same direction as the teacher. After hurrying through the stop sign, the driver then slowed to about ten miles per hour below the posted speed limit.

In deference to the little boy, the teacher who was driving declined to comment on the careless driver. The boy spoke up for her, though, and said, "That driver is a real dummy!" One of the teachers smiled and asked, "Is that what your father says when he is angry at a careless driver?"

"No," said the boy. "That is what my mother says. I am not permitted to say the bad words my father says."

* * *

The mother and father and the twelve children had just moved to town. They walked to the local Baptist church the following Sunday. The pastor honestly commented: "When I saw their name on the town's newcomers list, I thought they were Roman Catholic."

As the family filed into the church, people were amazed

as they counted the number of children filing by. A little girl turned to her younger brother and explained, "It's not really a family; it's really a birthday party."

* * *

The pastor's son, though only six years old, was already a seasoned veteran in moving from one town to another. On his first day of school he was more than prepared for the predictable questions other children would ask. So, the first and second questions were no surprise to him.

"Where does your father work?"

"He is a preacher."

"A preacher? Is that kind of tough on you to have a preacher for a father?"

"Not too much. My biggest problem is that he doesn't practice what he preaches."

* * *

Conversation overheard between two eight-year-old girls:

"You have to be a virgin to be baptized."

"No, you don't. I'm Assembly of God and *I've* been baptized."

* * *

The nine-year-old girl felt important. She was called upon to help Mommy teach four-year-old children in vacation church school.

During story time, the little children were in a trance at the perils of David facing Goliath, as narrated by the nine-year-old girl. The girl was deeply concerned, however. She knew how the story ended with Goliath being beheaded and she felt that would be too scary for the four-year-olds. The quick-thinking girl became the world's youngest redaction critic when she concluded the story this way: "And just before the rock hit Goliath, he was raptured and all the Philistines ran away."

Quality Time

The concept of "quality" time is a good idea. The problem with it is that many parents think quality time can always be fitted into a schedule. Sometimes parents need to be available for quality times that are not subject to scheduling. The sense of accomplishment over the first finger painting needs to be shared while the paint is wet; the joy of being at the head of the class in whatever activity needs to be shared in the uniqueness of the moment, rather than delayed for two or three days when 'quality' time rolls around again. Also, quality time does not always have to be unbridled joy. Occasionally, quality time needs to be a time of inquiry, or of confession.

For example, a four-year-old boy came in one day and asked his father if the two of them could go on a picnic. The father held a part-time job, a weekend pastorate, and was carrying a twelve-hour load of seminary studies. Despite his load of responsibilities, the father recognized that this would truly be quality time and wisely took advantage of it. His little boy had often brought his toys to Daddy's study and played quietly there, just to be near him for a while.

The boy had the picnic spot all picked out. It was a concrete table and bench in Forest Park just off University Drive in Fort Worth, Texas. As they sat there munching peanut butter and jelly sandwiches, the boy identified cars as the 5:00 traffic rolled by.

"Look, there goes a Chevy. There goes a Ford; there goes a Mustang. There goes a Buick. There goes a Pontiac. There goes my favorite, a Thunderbird!"

Daddy was deeply impressed. No doubt his little boy had heard the older boys in the student housing talk about cars. Daddy decided to tease the boy a little, and asked, "How do you *know* that's a Pontiac? It might be a Buick."

Bewildered by his father's ignorance of such things, the boy used his hands to make what, to him, were meaningful gestures and said, "If it were a Buick its taillights would be like this instead of like this!"

The father complimented his son on his astuteness. They sat in silence for a few moments. Daddy looked down at his little boy who was tugging on his short-sleeved shirt and hid his tears as his son asked, "Is this the kind of little boy you always wanted?"

Twenty-one years later, that father smiles through tears when he passes that picnic bench.

*   *   *

Or, consider the first-grade girl who needed some quality time as soon as she arrived home from school one day.

"Well, I guess I'm in trouble at school," she said as she sat down at the kitchen table and rested her chin in the palms of her hands.

Mommy sat down to hear more about this.

"Well, today at lunch, ummmm, this boy, he ran up to me in the lunch line when the teacher wasn't looking and kissed me on the cheek."

"I don't understand." said Mom. "How are you in trouble?"

"Well, I hate to tell you this, but this afternoon at recess I beat him up, so I guess I'm in trouble."

*   *   *

One evening while she was reading the Bible, her four-year-old daughter came up to ask, "Mommy, why do you read that book so much?"

She answered, "Because I love God and want to know all he has to tell me," thinking this would satisfy her small understanding.

The little girl giggled while replying, "Mommy, that book's not talking; you got to read the words."

Seeing that she was in for more explaining, the mother began to tell her daughter about God putting ideas in different men's minds so that they could write the book. As she talked she observed the puzzled look in her daughter's eyes turn to excited understanding. The youngster interrupted with, "Oh Mommy, I know, with the money I gave to Sunday school, God bought a pencil and wrote that Book!"

Chapter Two

━━━━━

A Time to Laugh . . .
The Hilarious Humor of Misused Words

Even the most polished person makes an occasional entertaining error. These faux pas range from getting words mixed, (or, as a friend used to say, "I got my mords wixed"), to innocently using the wrong word. On those occasions in which the polished and eloquent speaker errs with words, we find that to be humorous because it is such an unpredictable rare occurrence. On the other hand, we also laugh at people who, like Archie Bunker, almost constantly make verbal blunders. That is one of the marvels of humor; both its unpredictability and its predictability can be an occasion for laughter.

Think of the pomposity of a television network announcer, for instance, who ponderously states: "This program was taped before a *live* audience." Could there be any other kind of audience? The network announcer needs only to say, "Taped before an audience." Or, have you ever heard a preacher begin the invitation portion of a worship service with the solemn utterance, "If you are here today . . ."? The full sentence is usually something like, "If you are here today, and you are not a Christian, we invite you to accept Jesus now." The sentence would be improved by simply dropping the phrase, "If you are here today."

We all do and will make verbal faux pas on occasion. The best way to handle such a situation is to enjoy it. We must accept and enjoy our humanity, especially on humorous occasions.

A capacity to laugh at ourselves, and, therefore, laugh with others at the same time, greatly alleviates our embarrassment. To laugh at one's self is to accept one's humanity. (In fact, people who do not accept their humanity are being inhuman to themselves.) These stories include verbal bloopers — both written and oral — and are shared by those precious people who have that lovable capacity to laugh at themselves.

"Oops! That's Not What I Meant"

The preacher had just remarried. He had been a widower for several years. He bragged about his new wife frequently. The preacher seemed to be especially delighted with her numerous hobbies. One of her hobbies was collecting and restoring antiques. This prompted the preacher to say, "I didn't know what an antique *was* till I met Doris!"

* * *

The small print at the bottom of an order of worship bulletin was not encouraging.

"Those who must *heave* before the sermon is over are encouraged to do so quietly so as not to disturb the worship of others."

* * *

The wedding ceremony was well-planned, well-rehearsed, and proceeded smoothly — until the wedding vows, that is. In his best ministerial tone, the preacher asked, "Do you, Sue, take Tom to be your lawfully wedded husband? Will you love Tom, and cherish him as your husband so long as you both shall live?"

There was a long pause. The bride finally answered: "No, as a matter of fact I won't!"

It appeared to be one of those nightmarish situations any pastor would dread. "Have you changed your mind?" whispered the pastor. "Not at all," responded the bride. "The groom's name is John, not Tom!"

* * *

The advertisement in a denominational newsletter was for the sale of used church furniture. One line read:

"Small chairs for sale for children with straw seats."

* * *

Two young men walked the church aisle in response to an invitation at the end of the worship service. They both declared they had just received a divine call to preach. The pastor immediately announced, "We will put these calls to the test. One of these young men will preach one week from tonight and the other young man will preach two weeks from tonight!"

The church was crowded the next Sunday night. They were an expressive congregation anyway, but on this particular night they were especially so. The congregation wanted to show their support for the budding new preacher. Many of them were on their feet with rapturous expressions on their faces. Most of them were prepared to shout an encouraging amen after the first sentence of the young man's first sermon.

The preacher seemed self-assured and relaxed. He looked at the congregation, raised the Bible high and vigorously announced, "Tonight I will preach on the much-neglected doctrine of circumcision!" As he rattled off his scriptural references, he realized the congregation was quiet and most of them had a stupefied expression on their faces. The preacher observed, "I can see that this is truly a neglected doctrine. Most of you look like you've never even heard of it, but I am here to tell you that all good Christians have been circumcised. You take Miz _____ here, she's a good Christian! *She's been circumcised!*"

The preacher immediately started reading his text for the sermon. When he finished, he realized that not only was the congregation not offering their usual vocal support, they were not even looking at him. In fact, he noted they were not even looking at each other. He quickly surmised the problem and chided the congregation:

"I can't believe how little you people know about the Bible! I perceive you don't even know what circumcision is, so I will define it for you! That's right, bury your faces in your hands! You ought to be ashamed! That's good, some of you are crying! That's the way it ought to be! All right now, here is the definition of circumcision — look up here now so you can see." The "preacher" slapped his forehead and declared, "Circumcision is the removal of the forehead skin. That's how God marks his people!"

Shortly after the "sermon," after a quick conference with the two "preachers," the pastor announced: "The other young man will not be preaching next Sunday night. Both of them are leaving to attend seminary this week."

* * *

A revision of the bylaws was submitted to the church. In the personnel section, the pastor's duties included this statement: ". . . shall sacrificially minister to the church and perish."

* * *

The preacher had the unfortunate habit of making long pauses (ten seconds or more) to check his sermon notes. The pauses almost always occurred in the middle of a sentence. The congregation found themselves listening for which sentences would be misconstrued by a misplaced pause. The congregation voted these two sentences, with pauses, as their favorites:

"Two years ago when I was living . . . in another town," and

"Last night I witnessed to a termite . . . control man."

* * *

The church newsletter had a special announcement about a change in the frequency of worship services:

"Next Sunday, May 26, our church will begin having only one morning worship at 11:00 a.m. which will continue through the summer months."

* * *

The pastor hurried to a deacon's home. The deacon and his wife had been bound, gagged and terrorized by burglars. Their daughter found them several hours later. The deacon and his wife were shaken by the experience, but they had not been otherwise physically abused. As word of the trauma spread around the community, someone thought to notify the pastor. When the pastor arrived he ministered to the family in a marvelous way. By the time he left, everyone felt better. Everyone, that is, except the pastor who could hardly believe his incredible string of blunders.

As soon as he arrived at the deacon's house, the pastor walked directly to the deacon and blurted: "I'm glad they got your belongings, but I'm sorry they didn't get you!" As the deacon's bewilderment changed to laughter, the pastor realized what he had said and apologized profusely. The deacon insisted he understood and suggested the pastor visit with his wife who was still emotionally distraught. Thus, the preacher walked into blunder number two.

The wife was surrounded by relatives and friends. She saw

the pastor and said, "I must talk to you. Now!" The only room
that offered any privacy was the bathroom. They went in there
and shut the door. She sat on the edge of the bathtub, he sat
on the commode. She poured her heart out. She wished she
could have killed the burglars, where was God in all of this,
etc. When they stood up to leave, he, out of habit, flushed
the commode. Of course it was heard throughout the house.
As he left the bathroom, he tried not to notice the quizzical
expressions on everyone's face. Again, bewilderment changed
to laughter, and a red-faced pastor sought another way to
minister.

The pastor saw a distant relative of the family and moved
over to him and introduced himself, "And is your wife here?"
asked the pastor. "Oh, no, my wife has died and gone to
heaven."

"I'm sorry to hear that — no I mean I'm glad to hear that
— no I am sorry to hear that . . . do you have any idea what
I mean?"

"Pastor," said the deacon, "you are the most unusual, best
pastor we've ever had."

* * *

Quote from an advertisement:
"Our bookstore has been converted from new Christian
to used Christian."

* * *

The college student wrote a thank-you note to her Sunday church school teacher who had remembered her birthday:
"You always cease to amaze me."

* * *

The pastor had an inspiration! He ran to the choir rehearsal room that Wednesday night. He interrupted the rehearsal to say that at a certain point in next Sunday's sermon it would be good if the choir would "unanimously and *spontaneously*" begin to sing a certain hymn. The choir obediently followed the pastor into the sanctuary and listened as he rapturously shared a portion of his sermon.

At the assigned place, the choir tentatively began to sing. Finally, the "rehearsal" was over. The pastor, never strong on the use of words, thanked the weary choir for taking time to "rehearse our spontaneity." When Sunday came, the pastor inspired a different sort of spontaneity. His cue sentence was to include the word "paraclete," which he called "parakeet."

* * *

The list of activities for the week in the church bulletin included this item:

"Thursday at 5:00 p.m. there will be a meeting of the Little Mothers Club. All wishing to become little mothers will please meet the minister in his study."

* * *

The pastor who could "rehearse spontaneity" was no more adept in the use of words on any other occasion. While introducing a female guest, he assured the congregation that she ". . . is one of the few women leaders in the denomination with whom he has not been intimate." Later, prompted by the female guest, he announced he meant to say ". . . one of the few women leaders in the denomination with whom he had not been acquainted."

The pastor was a walking equal-opportunity malapropism. In the children's sermon he gravely suggested that God is like

"a giant umbrella and all the denominations are his outhouses."
The parents assured the children that he meant to say
"outposts."

* * *

A note on the church bulletin board:

"An open invitation to all those who would like to sin
in the choir. This Sunday our special will be 'Love Divine All
Lovers Excelling'."

* * *

The family had been looking forward to living in Little
Rock again. They had lived there before and enjoyed themselves. Now they had returned to the city they loved and to
the same job that had been left behind years ago. When they
rejoined their beloved church, they were reintroduced to the
congregation. The reintroduction went well until the pastor
observed that the husband and father of the family was returning to his former job. "Ah," said the pastor, "I see that he
is back for his second stench."

* * *

Found in the suggestion box of a metropolitan Lutheran
church:

"Could we have more freedom in our worship and less
emphasis on lethargy?"

* * *

The sermon was based on the healing miracles of Christ.
The preacher was renowned for his scholarly, yet

warm-hearted sermons. This was achieved, the pastor said, by bringing Bible characters to life. True to his teaching, the pastor dramatized a "conversation" between Jesus and numerous persons that needed physical healing. The sermonic "conversation" went like this:

"Blind people, can you see?"
"No, Jesus, we can't see!"
"Lame people, can you walk?"
"No, Jesus, we can't walk!"
"Deaf people, can you hear?"
"No, Jesus, we can't hear!"

* * *

Sentence in a sermon from Judges 3:
"As we can imagine the assassination did kill Eglon, so he took off, locking the doors to the room behind him."

Same sermon:
"That it might appear how happy the nation was in the Judges, it is here shown how unhappy they were when there was none."

Same sermon, final quote:
"She drove a spike through the sleeping Sesua's head, making him an example of earthly-mindedness."

* * *

The text was James 3. The sermon, predictably, was on "the tongue." The pastor knew what he meant, but did not consider how his words would sound. The pastor, therefore, was confused when the people chuckled at this sentence: "Long-tongued people (gossips) became long-taled people."

* * *

Business was slow at one stand at the church carnival. A few people came by to talk, but they did not stay long and no one wanted to buy anything. Finally, the monsignor came by with two jars of paint. He explained, "If I adjust one letter on this sign, your business will pick up quickly." Sure enough, business was good the rest of the evening. Her curiosity piqued, one worker went out to inspect the monsignor's work. Only then did she realize someone had posted the wrong sign on their booth. The monsignor had simply changed an 'F' to a 'C.' Now the sign read, "Concession Stand."

* * *

The pastor had wanted the big-name preacher to speak in his church for a long time. In his enthusiastic introduction of the guest preacher, the pastor claimed, "I have known and appreciated the work of this man in a special way and I want to assure you that when it comes to preaching, this man stands next to nothing! No! I mean stands next to none!"

The pastor, much abashed but not daunted, took the resulting laughter with great dignity. Then to restore the proper atmosphere to the service, he admitted: "Well, I messed that up pretty well. But let me guarantee you that after this man preaches, you will be glad when it's over!"

* * *

It was time for church announcements. There would be a conference for international students convening soon. Housing was needed, so the pastor advised: "Anyone who would like to share their bed with an international student, please call the church office."

* * *

The pastor was known as a cut-up. This Wednesday night,

however, he was deadly serious. It took a while, but he finally convinced his congregation that ". . . there is a burden on my heart tonight." The pastor asked everyone that could to please stay for a special prayer session. He advised those who could not stay for a long session to please leave now. A few folks left. He advised those who remained to cluster in the front, center pews. They did.

There was a hush over the congregation. The pastor lost his congregation, however, when he intoned: "I want you to put your seat over the head in front of you . . ."

* * *

The order of worship vividly stated:

"Words of Medication . . . . . . Pastor."

* * *

The preacher was not known for an ecumenical spirit. The congregation was a little shocked, then, that the subject of the sermon was "The Baptist Faith and Methodist." The shock wore off as the congregation deduced that the preacher meant to say, "Baptist Faith and Message."

The shock returned, however, during an illustration. The preacher had witnessed an automobile accident recently, and declared: "I shall never forget with a cracked tailbone and a concussion, the wailing moan of the accident victim . . ."

* * *

Sign in front of a church:

"The sinside of our church is being remodeled. Please, bear with us as we go through this tedious process."

* * *

During a business meeting, a deacon said, "I move we give a moratorium to our guest preacher." Fortunately, someone else moved that the guest preacher be given an honorarium.

* * *

The former pastor reassures everyone that his sermon on demons had nothing to do with his resignation. It was a good, biblical sermon. The problem was that about halfway through the sermon the word "demon" became "deacon." The *former* pastor reassures everyone that a slip of the tongue had nothing to do with his resignation. Someday, he will reassure even himself.

* * *

The chaplain officiating at the wedding service meant to say, "I now pronounce this couple lawfully joined together." He should have simply said, "I now pronounce you man and wife," but, no, he had to be more formal than that. What he did say was, "I now pronounce this couple joyfully loined together."

* * *

The following half-page ad appeared in a metropolitan newspaper:

A January To Remember
Featuring
A Contemporary Harpist
A prominent preacher from London
Renounced musicians

* * *

Sign in front of a church:

Morning Worship at 11:00
Text: Romans 3:23 ("For all have sinned and fallen short
of the glory of God")
Sermon: God Will Take Care of Our Falling Shorts

Chapter Three

———

The Rollicking Humor of Unexpected Events

The events that catch us off guard are often replete with humor. When these unpredictable events take place during what is supposed to be a serious moment, the humor is magnified. How much more serious can we be than during a church service? Whether it be worship, wedding, ritual, or a time of teaching, there seems to be a limit to how serious we will permit ourselves to be. When something unpredictable happens, most of us are more than eager to break the solemnity of the moment with healthy, vigorous laughter.

There are people who see this eagerness to laugh during what should be a serious time as inappropriate. The view taken here is that it is not only appropriate, but healthy to laugh at unpredictable events, even during what is ordinarily a rather serious moment. Many healthy congregations find that laughter does not distract from Christian growth, but actually enhances Christian growth. "Healthy" laughter usually occupies only a few moments of an entire service. Those few moments, however, often pave the way for the "serious" portion of the service to have its full impact.

Sorry, Wrong Church

The guest preacher was late, but by just a few minutes.

He jumped out of the taxi and ran to the front entrance. In the foyer to the auditorium he donned his clerical robe. He could hear the congregation singing and, by reading the hymn board at the front of the church, he knew it was the first hymn. He paused in the foyer till the congregation started the last stanza; he marched smartly down the aisle. As the stanza ended he had reached the pulpit and led the congregation in prayer. When the "Amen" was said, he turned around and found a seat beside the pastor on the platform. As the second hymn began, the pastor leaned toward the guest preacher and asked, "Who are you?" It was then that the guest preacher realized he was in the wrong church! On the way out, he noticed the church sign advertising the title of the sermon as "How to Help the Lost Find Their Way." Taking the title to heart, the guest preacher returned to the auditorium, and asked if any-one would be willing to give him directions to the church where he was supposed to be. Someone did, and in fact drove him to the nearby church where an anxious pastor was pac-ing the sidewalk, alternately praying that the guest would ar-rive, and preparing a new sermon in the event he did not arrive.

* * *

There are as many stories of preacher and guest preachers arriving at the wrong church as there are churches. A Southern Baptist missionary recalls that on the west side of Fort Worth, Texas, a Southern Baptist church and a Church of Christ build-ing were virtually side-by-side. The missionary recalls walk-ing down the aisle of the church after the service started, keenly observed by the congregation. He slowly put things together. There was no instrumental accompaniment to the music; the Lord's Supper would be observed; the prayer of invocation referred to a minister as minister instead of pastor. The mis-sionary silently prayed that the invocation would last long enough for him to walk back up the aisle. It was, he did, and the Southern Baptist church was quickly located.

* * *

The guest preacher left home Sunday morning in plenty of time to arrive at a church in Mount Vernon, and so he did. Only then did he reread the letter inviting him to preach, and so, only then did he realize that he was invited to speak in *Vernon*, not Mount Vernon. He scrambled to a telephone, called the church in Vernon, told them he would arrive in time for the sermon. There was no way, said the church member, that he could drive from Mount Vernon to Vernon in time to preach; it was just too far. At 11:20 a.m., the guest preacher walked into the church at Vernon, five minutes before he was scheduled to preach. Some day, when the statute of limitations runs out, he will share with us just how fast he drove. A message, though, to anyone who may have been on the road between Mount Vernon and Vernon that Sunday morning: the "fool" who sped by you was just another preacher trying to get to the correct church.

Sorry, Wrong Preacher

The man was in the correct church. In fact he sat in the same center pew every Sunday wearing the hearing aid he wore only at church. However, it was not a hearing aid. What it was, was an earplug to a transistor radio he carried in his inside coat pocket. He did not like the preaching of the preacher currently assigned to his church. Rather than change churches or denominations, he listened to the services of another church on his transistor radio while his own pastor was preaching.

The radio preacher was told about his "secret" listener, and, for whatever reason, made reference to him in that morning's radio sermon. The man was so pleased that he startled himself and everyone else in the worship service when he suddenly stood up, clapped his hands, and shouted, "Well, I'll be! I do think he is talking about me!"

His pastor recovered enough to say, "I assure you, I did not have you specifically in mind, but I am happy for you to make such fervent application of my sermon." The sermon subject at the church was "Thou shalt not covet thy neighbor's wife." The man says he does not remember the subject of the radio sermon.

Sorry, No Vision

Every church has its resident "sleepy head." Some people just cannot sit still that long without dropping off to sleep. Almost every church has a favorite story about their "sleeper." One of these heavy-lidded folk shares this story about himself:

"When I drifted off, as I usually do, everything was fine. The preacher was preaching, and I was seated between my wife and daughter. While I was asleep, as I later learned, the power went out throughout the neighborhood. The preacher calmed the congregation and suggested they each keep their seat. He would continue the sermon, since he did not use notes, and the congregation could remain seated until the lights came back on, or until the end of the service.

"I awakened to pure darkness. The preacher's voice was calm and strong. No problem there. I scratched my nose and couldn't even see my hand! I reached over to my daughter, put my hand on her head. I felt her head turn toward me and then back to the preacher. No problem there. I moved my other hand toward my wife. When our hands touched, she squeezed mine tenderly and let go. No problem there.

"But I had a problem. I blinked hard, massaged my eyelids, shook my head back and forth. Desperation was growing all the time. Finally, I couldn't stand it any longer. I was sweating through my clothes! I had to do something! So, I stood up and screamed, "I'm blind, God help me, I'm blind!"

"My wife and daughter brought me under control, the congregation laughed, and I learned two things. One, sleepers should always have first choice on the back pews so they can leave as quickly as possible in case they embarrass themselves. Two, sleepers do not need to have stories made up about them; they do very well on their own, thank you."

Could You Make An Exception?

The pastor search committee was particularly interested in one prospective pastor. A letter of recommendation of this pastor had them a little perplexed. The person making the recommendation wrote:

"Dear Friends:

I am happy to recommend Brother _____ to you. He is a fine, decent man and would make you a wonderful pastor. He is happy where he is, and has been happy wherever he has served. Despite his present happiness, I definitely feel led of God to recommend him to you. I assure you that if I did not feel a strong sense of divine leadership in this matter, I would not be wasting your time with this recommendation. Please, pray about this matter, and let me know if you have any questions.

Sincerely,

_____

P.S. If it should turn out that he is not interested in your church, I am."

* * *

The long-distance call was for the chairman of the pastor search committee. The caller inquired, "Did you receive my application to become pastor of your church?"

"Yes, we did," replied the chairman.

"Have you decided on me one way or the other?"

"Yes, we did," replied the chairman again.

"Your voice sounds as if the decision was negative. Let me see. You should have no problem with my offer to buy the church for $20,000, or with my installing my son as the associate pastor . . ."

"Well, we . . ." said the chairman.

"I know," interrupted the caller. "My wife is a Jehovah's Witness. That bothers you doesn't it?"

"Well, yes, but . . ." said the chairman.

"Just as I thought," interrupted the caller again. "Tell you what I will do. I will leave her if you will accept me as pastor. Does that help?"

"Not really," said the chairman as he disconnected the phone.

* * *

The Methodist pastor took the phone call at home. The female caller apologized for the interruption, but her mother was admitted to the hospital that afternoon. Her mother was desperately ill. Would the pastor mind visiting her right away.

"I do not mind visiting her tonight," said the pastor. "Tell me her name." The caller gave him the name which he recognized at once as a prominent Baptist lady.

"But your mother is a Baptist, and I am a Methodist pastor. Listen, I know the Baptist pastor, so let me call him and tell him about your mother."

"Oh, no," said the somewhat anxious caller. "Mother has a contagious disease and we love our pastor and we don't want him to catch it; that's why we want you to go."

Help Yourself, Preacher

The corpulent visitor to the nursing home always claimed to be visiting for the church. The senior citizens were wise to him. They knew he also came to help them consume food sent to them by their families. They were all disappointed when he refused to visit them any more after once consuming a bowl of peanuts while visiting one elderly couple.

He had complimented an elderly couple on the peanuts. The couple assured him that he was welcome to them, since they could not eat peanuts. However, they shared with him later, they did enjoy licking the chocolate off of those particular peanuts.

Sorry, Too Much Planning

The chaplains had elaborate plans for a worship service to impress the general. There would be a large procession. First would come the flag bearers, next the choir, followed by the orchestra. The choir and orchestra would file in two-by-two, watching the flag bearers for direction.

The procession began. The flag bearers marched to the front and then to each side as they were directed. The choir was in, and so was some of the orchestra — *some* of the orchestra! The flag bearers moved back up the side aisles to make more room for the orchestra. The flag bearers found themselves back at the front door. Still, some of the orchestra was outside. The flag bearers moved down the center aisle again. Now the procession was squeezed into a four-by-four procession. Finally, everyone was in.

Was the general impressed? Only if bewildered is synonymous with impressed.

Remember That Wedding When . . .

Military chapels often have weddings scheduled one after the other. It would be easy to get confused.

The Chaplain Major officiating at the wedding declared, "If anyone knows just cause why this couple should not wed, speak now or forever hold your peace."

The answer came from the back of the chapel. "I know just cause," asserted the airman as he strode smartly to the

"I object . . . I think!"

altar. He stopped suddenly and said, "Sorry, Chaplain, wrong wedding. It must be the next bride I object to," and he smartly strode to the back of the chapel again.

* * *

The best man at the military wedding was a civilian Baptist preacher. He either forgot himself or just had to say something. As the chaplain instructed the couple to build a Christian home, the best man suddenly blurted, "Amen! That's right! And Point Two is . . . uh, excuse me, Chaplain. Carry on, please."

* * *

The groom did not show up for the wedding. Six weeks later, the groom called the bride. "I can't stand it!" he cried. "Please, tell me. How did you take it when I didn't show up?"

* * *

The young couple came by the parsonage to ask the pastor to perform their wedding. "We live in Houston," they told the pastor, "but she wants to be married in her home church. We won't be back until about an hour before the wedding. Will you do our wedding?" The pastor objected that there should be a rehearsal, but the couple assured him that it would be a simple say-the-vows-before-the-family ceremony.

Predictably, the ceremony grew all week. The pastor, who had been out of town all week, was horrified to find he would officiate at a large wedding ceremony with no rehearsal, rather than the simple ceremony he had anticipated. Again, the young couple assured the pastor, "Everyone knows where they are supposed to be and where they are supposed to stand. Don't worry about it."

Unlike the opera, which has often been said not to be *over* until the fat lady sings, the wedding doesn't *begin* until the fat lady sings. She sang. The pastor heard the organist begin processional music. The pastor led the groom, best man, and groomsmen out to the altar area of the church. The men were surprised to see the soloist standing there about to begin another song. The organist stopped the processional music and started accompaniment for "I Love You Truly." By this time, the soloist had retreated and the organist began the processional again. The pastor looked down the aisle for the bridesmaids, but instead he saw a line of people waiting to be seated by the ushers. Rather than leave, he signalled the ushers to hurry. They did. Then, the aisles were empty. The front door of the church was partially open. From what the pastor could see, the bridesmaids and the bride were standing on the front lawn enjoying some girl talk, unaware that the wedding ceremony was underway. The pastor stared at one of the girls, willing her to turn around and look at him. She did. Slowly she realized it was their time to march down the aisle. The organist, especially, was relieved not to have to play the processional again.

The bride and her father stopped near the first pew. The pastor, much relieved, asked, "Who gives this woman in holy matrimony?" He looked toward the father for a response. The father, however, seemed to be chewing on something, and was looking in another direction. Just before the pastor repeated the question, the father glanced at the pastor. The father stepped up to the pastor, and put his face in the pastor's face and in a high-pitched voice and with his right hand behind his right ear, said, "Speak up, Sonny, what did you say?" The pastor held the Bible up to hide his face and kept telling himself, "Don't laugh. If you laugh, the whole congregation will laugh." The pastor regained his composure, and asked the question again. This time the father answered, "I still didn't hear you, but I suppose you're asking that dumb preacher question and the answer is 'Her mother and I,' that's who. Who else do you think gives brides away, anyway."

"Don't laugh," the preacher said to himself . . .

A *Long* Introduction

For whatever reason, the retired preacher was called upon
to introduce the guest speaker at a church luncheon. The retired preacher was known to pray for 20-30 minutes. Some
people said that he prays as he eats — he does not know when
to quit. Once, during a long prayer, a child asked, "Why does
he keep on praying when the pastor keeps saying 'Amen'?"
On the occasion of the introduction, he walked behind the
chair of the guest speaker, put his hands on the shoulders of
the guest speaker and began the introduction which was as
long-winded as usual. Toward the end of the introduction,
which lasted twenty-eight minutes, the retired preacher seemed
confused. He paused, looked around the room, and said, "I
have forgotten why I am up here." "To introduce the guest
speaker," shouted the congregation. "Then, we have a
problem," said the retired preacher, "for I do not see our guest
speaker. Where is he?" "Under your chin," shouted the congregation. "Oh," said the retired preacher as he sat down, "the
guest speaker is well-known to all of us and needs no introduction."

Use Whatever Resources Available

It was Youth Sunday. The youth were in charge of all
the services. The youth pastor was positive that he should get
credit for everything that happened in the service that day.
He received one of the rewards of the pompous when he took
the white cloth off the Lord's Supper table and received due
credit when he saw an unopened jar of grape juice and an unopened box of crackers on the table.

Another congregation did not fare even that well during
another Youth Sunday. The youth pastor found the trays containing the Lord's Supper elements filled and ready. When it
was time for drinking "of the cup" the congregation simul-
taneously nearly gagged, as did the youth pastor. After the

service he went to the youth Lord's Supper committee to ask what was wrong with the grape juice. The explanation:

"Well, it was late and we didn't have any grape juice anywhere. We couldn't get to the store and back in time. Just then we heard an ice cream truck cruising the neighborhood. We stopped the truck and he sold us the grape syrup he uses for snow cones and we filled the glasses with that."

Remember the Baptism When . . .

During a baptismal service at a small town church north of Austin, Texas, a teenage boy who was afraid of water began thrashing as he was being immersed. He grabbed a curtain dividing the baptistry from a dressing room behind it. When the curtain came down it covered the pastor and the baptismal candidate and it gave the congregation a view of a man who had just been baptized, drying his bare back and oblivious to the fact that he was now visible to the congregation. A quick-thinking deacon turned off the lights to give the man a chance to hide until the curtain could be put up again. The deacon waited until the commotion in the baptistry died down and, confident that the naked man had wrapped a towel around himself and moved to another room, turned on the lights. The pastor and the teenage boy were leaving the baptistry. The man, however, stood facing the congregation with his hands on his hips wondering who turned off the lights.

* * *

The pastor had always sprinkled for "baptism." He had never immersed anyone. Nevertheless, an immersion was necessary, so he found a church that would let him use their baptistry. The congregation watched in awe as the pastor wrapped his arms around the person to be baptized and dunked both of them.

* * *

The young pastor stepped into the baptistry, turned his back to the congregation, and baptized each of the candidates. After the service his wife asked him why he baptized with his back to the congregation. "So that was what it was," said the young pastor, "I knew I was doing something wrong."

* * *

During these days in which football players are nicknamed "Refrigerator," the very large man who was to be baptized would have been called "The Kitchenette." He wanted to be baptized, but was desperately afraid of water. The minister, dwarfed by the large man, said his pronouncements and started to immerse the man. The man decided he would go down no further. The struggle continued for a few seconds with the man holding on to the rim of the baptistry. The enterprising minister kicked the legs of the man, put the man's head underwater and immediately the man fainted. The minister dragged the man out of the water muttering something about a beached whale. Not knowing that the baptistry microphone was still on, the revived, baptized man asked, "Did it work?" "I don't know," answered the minister, "I never did get your stomach baptized!"

Nature's Call

The presentation of the *Messiah* was lengthy as always — too lengthy for one man who felt "nature's call." He left his pew and walked down the aisle to some side doors to a hallway, where he would find a room where he could answer nature's call. The side doors were locked. It was a long way back up the aisle to the front door, so he decided to try the side door in the choir area. Up to the choir he marched, but there was no side door there. *Across* the choir he marched as they sang. Fortunately, there was a door and it was not locked. The choir and congregation relaxed. They relaxed too

soon. A soloist, whose microphone was on, warned everyone, "Good heavens! He's coming back!"

Never Get Your Cat Confused

The preacher would have done well to ignore the cat.
Somehow the cat found entrance into the church auditorium
and wandered up to the balcony. No one was seated in the
balcony. The cat climbed on the balcony railing and walked
back and forth. The preacher was disturbed and distracted. His
distraction with the cat caused him not to notice that at the
same time, a very large woman was leaving her seat in the middle of a pew. Near the aisle she got stuck. While the pastor
eyed the cat, the rest of the congregation eyed the heavy lady.
In exasperation, the pastor asked, "Will some of you ushers
help that old cat get out of here?"

At Last, She Laughed

The new pastor's wife was very timid. One lady declared
that she would make it "her project" to help the new pastor's wife "open up and learn how to laugh." Her project was
unsuccessful for several months. At a church social, the pastor's wife suddenly broke into hearty laughter. The lady who
had made it a project to teach the new pastor's wife to laugh
had finally succeeded. On the way to the church social, she
stopped at a convenience store to buy some panty hose. With
a logic that is unique to such persons, the lady decided to put
her panty hose on while she drove. Somewhere between traffic
lights she realized the panty hose were too short. Undaunted, she tugged until she felt some release. The new pastor's
wife was the first to notice that the lady was barefoot — the
feet of her panty hose had split and were located just above
her ankles.

So, Now We Know

The man was, professedly, a Bible-believin', church-attendin', total-abstainin' Baptist. One Friday night after a high school football game, the man and his wife, the pastor of the man's church and his wife, and another couple all went to a nice restaurant. The man praised the avocado dip served there. He declared that he had never eaten a dip as good as that avocado dip and couldn't wait to get some.

The orders were given to the waitress. She brought a tray of appetizers, but no avocado dip. She brought the soup, but no avocado dip. She brought the entree, but no avocado dip.

So the avocado dip fan asked her, "Look, where is our avocado dip? I was in here last week and we had the best avocado dip I had ever eaten. I see that other tables have avocado dip. Why don't we have avocado dip?"

"Sir," she replied, "we serve avocado dip only when you order a drink from the bar."

* * *

When Dr. Jimmie Nelson of Southwestern Seminary was a "preacher-boy" at Baylor, he and a classmate were invited to hold a weekend revival at a small country church southeast of Waco. After the Sunday morning service a little lady redundantly described herself as "the widow woman who was going to feed the preachers their lunch that day."

Jimmie said they literally walked into a Ma Kettle situation. Their hostess shoved chickens off the table, the plates and utensils were dirty, and they weren't real sure about what she dished out of the pot.

The two preacher boys ate enough, they thought, to be polite. They jumped into Jimmie's car and headed for a country store down the road and bought some cheese, cold cuts, crackers, soft drinks, cakes and fruit. They whiled away the afternoon under a shade tree at the church. That evening as the congregation gathered again for services, Jimmie heard one of the men ask their hostess if she had "the preachers over for lunch" that day. Jimmie said we couldn't face that lady again after she replied, "Yeah, but I guess I didn't fix anything they liked. They went to my daughter's store and like to bought it out."

* * *

The Presbyterian lady was accustomed to doing things in an orderly fashion. She joined a weekly Bible study group composed largely of Baptists. The Presbyterian lady was accustomed to a prayer book. The Baptists "just pray from the heart."

At the beginning Bible study session, the Presbyterian lady was called upon to lead a prayer for the group. She groped through her prayer book, but could not find *the* prayer for that occasion. She was certain she had heard one. She startled the rest of the group by saying, "If someone will get me started, I believe I could finish it."

Thus prompted, one Bible study group member volunteered, "Our Heavenly Father . . ."

* * *

It was one of those rare days on the plains of West Texas when the wind was not gusting. The sanctuary windows were open for the evening service of the Baptist Church. The preacher was well into his sermon when a bird flew through an open window behind him. The bird circled above the congregation and then swooped down through another open window and was gone. The preacher acknowledged that, sure enough, a bird had flown in and found its way out again and resumed his sermon.

This church, however, had a Mr. Five-by-Five (five feet tall and five feet wide) who tended to little details in the church. For some reason he left his seat and went to the window through which the bird had flown. As he reached up to close it his suspenders snapped and his trousers fell to his ankles. The man was not wearing underwear. The man grabbed his trousers, pulled them up to his waist and tiptoed out through a back door.

The preacher saw none of this. What he did see was a congregation that could barely hide its mirth. Grown men had to avoid each other's eyes lest they break into laughter. Dainty ladies held handkerchiefs over their mouths to stifle themselves. Kids had their heads down between their knees and were snickering as quietly as they could.

One member of the congregation said afterwards that they could have settled back into their dignified church manners if the preacher hadn't become irritated with them. The congregation had to literally explode with laughter when the pastor shouted, "C'mon, people. You've all seen a little birdie before!"

Chapter Four

The Quaint Humor
on a Seminary Campus

The stereotype of a seminary campus is of a staid, stolid, solemn, serious place where great thoughts are uttered in ways that even other theologians cannot understand. This stereo- type is true. Only on a seminary campus can one be enthralled by such lofty discussions as how many angels may stand on the head of a pin, or how many demons may be hidden in the cavities of a block of Swiss cheese, or when the Lord will return, or how to find a church with a brick parsonage and all utilities paid. In such a setting there surely is no room for laughter.

That part of the stereotype is not true.

A seminary is like any other institution. A seminary is also unlike any other institution. A seminary has all of the interpersonal tensions that may be found on any campus. There are tensions between students and students, between faculty and faculty, between administrators and administrators and between any combination of the above, just as there are in any institution. In seminaries these tensions are minimized and sometimes nullified by a sense of Christian grace. Two or more persons who may have raised their voices at one another during a meeting are often seen leaving arm-in-arm. At one moment their tensions were intensely felt; at a later moment, when these tensions were mollified, they became the best of friends again.

Both the tensions and the grace, the problems and the high

character of the individuals involved, are the seed beds of humorous situations. In the midst of all its solemnity, the halls of seminaries reverberate with laughter as often as any place in the world.

A Word not Fitly Spoken

The student had not only raised his hand, but was waving frantically. It was the first class of the first day of the semester — 8:00 a.m. The professor thought to himself, "A frantic student already! He can't be asking to be excused — the bell hasn't even rung yet. Maybe he is an apple polisher . . ."

Impatiently, the student nearly shouted, "Sir, I have an urgent prayer request!"

"Okay, Son. Hold onto it. I will call on you as soon as the bell rings."

Finally, the bell rang. As promised, the prof called upon the student to share his urgent prayer request. Somehow, all of the frenetic energy of a few minutes ago left the student. Instead, he stood slowly and with dignity. After establishing eye contact with the class, he ponderously stated: "I have an urgent prayer request. A friend of mine is going into the hospital tomorrow for an autopsy."

The bemused class held their mirth until the professor said dryly, "Let us know if everything comes out all right . . ."

* * *

The same student brought two other befuddled prayer requests to the same class. The next request was for a missionary family who would soon be home on "parole." His third request of note was for the class to remember him in prayer because, "I am going before a church this Sunday in lieu of a call." To which the professor responded, "That may be the most prophetic thing you ever say." And so it was. To this day that student is still perplexed that the class voted him the future preacher most likely to be able to charge admission to his sermons.

* * *

A "rookie" professor in the School of Church Music was assigned to teach a class of theology students a course titled "Ministry of Music II." The new prof was a genuine, warm-hearted person. This fact guaranteed that he would have a rocky time in Ministry of Music II. The "guarantee" was effected in the third week of the four-week course.

The new prof invited a veteran prof to demonstrate singing without accompaniment. As the rookie professor introduced the soloist, he became enmeshed in his own graciousness. The class was already snickering at the grimaces of the soloist as he sat through the extended, glowing introduction to what was, after all, a rather routine assignment. The class absolutely guffawed when the professor concluded his introduction by touchingly stating, "I can truly say you are going to be glad when this is over."

A Word that is Fitly Spoken

The crusty old professor had been teaching Philosophy of Religion for a long time. His lengthy tenure and his own intellectual brilliance made it difficult for him to teach the introductory course in his field. He began his introductory course with an apology for all the times he would be sarcastic in the semester ahead. True to his word, he would admonish students for missing an answer on a quiz ("You must be kidding me — my grandchildren could answer that question!"), for not comprehending the assigned reading ("You are familiar with the disciplines of reading, are you not?"), but most especially for being tardy to a class ("Behold, we have a latter day saint among us!").

One day the class of 130 theology students was taken

aback when the bell rang and their professor was not there! Had he, too, become a latter day saint? The unwritten rule of respect was to wait ten minutes before "taking a walk." Five minutes later, the professor came limping into the classroom.

His speech was slurred as he explained, "I sprained my ankle while playing basketball with my son, yesterday. Also, my mouth is broken out with some ulcers, so I'm having trouble speaking clearly, but . . ." But before he could finish his sentence, someone yelled, "Sounds like hoof and mouth disease!"

To his credit, he patiently waited through the several minutes it took for the eruption of laughter to die away.

* * *

The new seminary student was also relatively new to the Christian life. He spent a lot of time observing the behavior of professors and students in a search for role models in various situations. He was fairly certain that he liked his archaeology professor. The professor talked and acted like a "regular guy" and this appealed to the student.

A few minutes before class one day, a group of "apple polishers" were discussing ways to "butter up" the professor in order to manipulate him for an 'A' in the course.

"Doctor," they said as the professor approached, "we just want to tell you how much we enjoy this course. We find ourselves talking about you all the time. In fact, we spend so much time on this course, we have neglected our other studies."

"Oh, no," thought the student, "he's buying this pack of lies. He appears to be downright pleased!"

The student's confidence was restored when the professor smiled and said, "Sounds like a bunch of bull to me."

* * *

Do you know what a professor is? A Baptist college professor wanted to know if his freshmen students knew, so he took a survey. The college professor suspects that at least some of the answers were provided by upperclassmen.

1. He is the fellow who talks in the sleep of others
2. A textbook wired for sound
3. The one who gets the contents of *his* notebook into the notebooks of students by means of a ballpoint pen, without passing through the minds of either
4. A person who can go down deeper, stay down longer and come up drier than anyone you know
5. A person who dried up by degrees
6. A person who, when knocked down in the hall by a student rushing to class, finds it necessary to inquire in which direction he had been going. When he is told he was headed for the library, he replies, "That means I have had breakfast, doesn't it?"

* * *

The seminary president detested long-winded telephone calls. When one could get him on the telephone, he would wait till it was finally his turn to talk and say, "Now let me make a suggestion . . ." Then he would disconnect the call and leave the office for a few minutes with these instructions to his secretary: "If that person should call back, tell them we were disconnected."

* * *

A preaching professor had just celebrated his seventy-ninth birthday by taking a new bride. He had been a widower for one year and one day when he married. One day in class he gave a great lecture on the responsibilities of a husband to his wife. When he finished, one student asked the seventy-nine-year-old professor, "Sir, how old does a man have to be before he stops looking at pretty girls?"

His reply: "He's got to be older than seventy-nine!"

* * *

W. T. Conner was a great theology teacher. Many of his books are used as textbooks long after his death. Conner was also a great teacher who knew how to communicate. He had a biting sense of humor as well. In his lectures on fore-ordination and free will he would illustrate with an imaginary person who was a strict "Calvinist." This person believed that God foreordained *everything* that happened, including how often he would inhale and exhale. One day this man was reading and walking down a hallway. He did not notice that he was approaching a stairway. He fell hard. When others came to his assistance, he was heard to mutter, "Well, God, I am glad you got that over with . . ."

* * *

A student one day interrupted Dr. Conner to ask a question. Dr. Conner answered, "I do not know the answer to your question." The student then proceeded to tell what he thought the answer should be. The good professor interrupted him this time, by saying, "Son, I didn't say you don't know; I said I don't know!"

Are We Still Friends?

Cal Guy moved from Tennessee to Texas to attend seminary. As it turned out, he had an illustrious career in Texas and never returned to live in Tennessee. He must have wondered on at least one occasion if he were in the right place. His Hebrew professor explained the nature of the various Hebrew verb tenses, and concluded by saying, "We need preaching in the *piel* (the verb tense with great emphasis), not in the *qal*" (the verb tense that is passive and pronounced "Cal"). "I tell you," the professor yelled, "We need men to preach in the piel; I don't have any use for those qal guys!" A few years later, Guy got his revenge. He brought a missionary who could speak modern Hebrew to meet his Hebrew professor. Guy said, "Doc, you are a linguist, so I want you to identify the language this missionary is about to speak." The missionary spoke in modern Hebrew. The professor listened attentively and then said, "That would be a Chinese dialect." Guy never let his Hebrew professor live it down.

* * *

The widower professor spoke glowingly about a lady he admired. A student teased the elderly professor and said, "Why Doctor, I do believe you are in love. Are you going to propose to this lady?"

"I guess not," the professor said after thinking about it for a while. "She has a Student Union spirit, but a Women's Missionary Union figure."

* * *

The professor called the roll on the first day of class. He looked over the class first as if he were trying to locate someone. Eventually, he said, "Will Miss Jesse stand up, please?" "Miss Jesse" turned out to be a mister. The professor was embarrassed, and said, "Why didn't you tell me you were a boy?" The student retorted, "I thought you would give me a better grade if you thought I were a girl!" The professor, now a little less flustered, said, "I probably already have."

* * *

L. R. Elliott was a pleasant man most of the time, but was an "old grouchy, grizzly bear" when he taught Greek. For years stories abounded about his tough-mindedness on details of the language. Students said that if they left off an iota subscript, he would send you there.

Years later a couple of his former students had an opportunity to 'roast' Dr. Elliott. Said one, "I don't know any Greek but all that I do know has been taught to me by Dr. Elliott." In tandem, the other former student added: "I had no trouble with his Greek; it was his English I couldn't understand."

Another of Elliott's students later carried on the Elliott tradition at the same school. However, a new student generation felt the freedom to take their complaints to the seminary president. For years the president loved to share this conversation with a group of complaining students:

"This Greek professor is too hard on tests!"

"How hard is he?"

"Well, if you guess at an answer and miss it, he counts off three points. If you just plain miss it, he counts off two points. If you get the right answer he is kind enough to count off only one point."

* * *

Seminary students are always looking for ways to impress their professors. They often succeed one way or another. The New Testament professor told his class that Luther and Calvin had little regard for the book of Revelation. "By the way," he asked, "how many of you have copies of Calvin's commentary on Revelation?" One man seized the opportunity and raised his hand when he saw that no one else in class had his hand up. He turned to the professor to say, "Man, I'm really unique!" To which the professor said, "You have no idea how unique you are. Calvin did not write a commentary on Revelation."

Did I Hear You Right?

The dean of the school of theology teased a faculty member: "You must have some malady. Every time I need a volunteer to take on an extra responsibility, you are always the first to volunteer. I know that the little bit of extra pay involved can't be the only reason you're taking on so many extra jobs. What gives with you anyway?"

The faculty member looked the dean in the eye and said, "I wasn't going to tell anyone, but, yes, I do have a malady that necessitates generating all the extra income I can get."

The dean, chiding himself for making light of what was apparently a serious problem, said, "Oh, no. I'm so sorry to hear this. Do you mind sharing with me the nature of your problem?"

"Oh, Dean, since you asked I will tell you. Actually, it is not a private nor an uncommon malady. I am suffering from maltuition."

"Malnutrition! Man, you're not suffering from malnutrition!"

"No, Dean, I didn't say *malnutrition*, I said *maltuition* — I have a daughter in college."

* * *

At a reception for new students, glowing comments were made about a professor. "He is the Socrates of the seminaries; he is the Einstein of theology; he is the Billy Graham of preaching; he is the Plato of academics; and the Clark Gable of the faculty . . ." His wife's voice interrupted at this point to say, "Not at home."

* * *

For years the professor opened every class the same way. First he would say, "Let us pray." Immediately after the prayer, he would begin the lecture with, "Friends, today I want to speak to you about . . ." One morning he raised his hand to call for quiet and to begin the prayer, and said, "Friends, today I want to talk to you about . . ."

You may suppose that this shows he was a typical absent-minded professor. It does not show that at all. When confronted with this story, the professor rather haughtily responded. "That just shows that I am completely biblical and orthodox and fundamental. When I said, 'Friends,' I was simply being an Evangelical Trinitarian."

* * *

The two professors were having a "friendly" debate. Professor Bill concluded by saying, "Really, David, there's not a hair's breadth difference in us." David, not at all comforted, shot back, "Bill, I'm grateful for whatever difference there is!"

* * *

These days there are more women taking preaching classes. Not too long ago that was almost unheard of. This story occurred in that not-too-long-ago time.

One day the female preaching student went home and asked her husband to help her with some odds and ends while she finished a sermon. Things did not go so well. She was having trouble writing the sermon. Time dragged by and her husband, a pastor, offered to prepare supper.

About that time, the telephone rang. Their teenage daughter answered the phone. It was the chairman of the deacons. He wanted to speak to "the Mrs."

"Mother is busy," said the girl, "preparing her sermon." Thinking that the girl was teasing him, the man replied, "And I suppose your father is preparing supper."

"How did you know?" asked the girl in surprise.

* * *

The student was breathless. He had taken the steps two at a time. He ran down the hallway so fast, he over ran the

"My wife is going to have a baby! Is that all right?"

professor. He turned around and cried out, "Professor, I've been looking for you! My wife is going to have a baby! Is it all right?"

Later the professor realized that the student was asking if it was all right if he missed class that day.

* * *

Student to preaching professor: "I am not interested in Bible study. I just want to work with doctrine."

"I am thoroughly confused," answered the professor. "How do you do doctrine without Bible study?"

"Here is a sermon I preached last Sunday," offered the student. "You can see how I handled doctrine without bothering with tedious Bible study."

The professor pondered the sermon for a long time and then informed the student. "When you do a Bible study on this text, you will have *two* sermons on this text."

* * *

There was a denominational controversy about liberalism in the seminaries that caused lots of tension during the biannual trustees meetings. A new professor, eager to please and eager to be accepted, introduced himself to one of the "veteran" trustees. The trustee looked at the new professor quizzically and said, "You must be all right, I've never heard of you."

* * *

It was a difficult committee assignment. Each of the faculty members was emotionally involved in several areas of their deliberations. They spoke frankly and tried hard to agreeably disagree. Week-by-week the tensions built in every meeting. They admitted they were tired. Finally, they realized none of them would be friends for some time after their committee assignments were completed.

At the beginning of one of the tedious, emotionally drain-
ing meetings, the chairman called upon one of the committee
members to lead the committee in prayer. The faculty member prayed a positive prayer that each of them would be able
to set aside personal concerns and have a vision of what they
could do to help the kingdom of God. He closed his prayer
by saying, "Especially in these last meetings, let us have such
a vision. Amen."

Right on the heels of the amen, one committee member
asserted, "I take issue with your saying 'these last meetings.'
I think we have lots of work ahead of us, yet." To which
another committee member said, "I second that!"

The bewildered committee member who had voiced the
prayer turned to the chairman and asked, "Is proposing an
amendment to my prayer a proper agenda item?"

"Revenge is Mine," Saith . . .

Professor Bill took his recreation as seriously as he did his
theology. Professor Tom was one of the faculty pranksters.
Bill suspected it was Tom who suggested one day that Bill's
class sing Happy Birthday to their professor. Of course, it was
not Bill's birthday. Whether it was for this or some other
prank, Bill decided he would take revenge. Once a week Bill
and Tom went to the YMCA to swim or to play water polo.
Bill decided that he would give Tom a good dunking.

Bill hurriedly undressed and headed for the obligatory
shower before entering the pool. Unsuspecting Tom took his
time. Bill, wearing only his shower cap, waited just outside
the shower door to the pool area. Bill planned to jump on
Tom's back and ride him down to the water and give him the
dunking he felt Tom deserved.

Meanwhile, back in the locker room, another man came
into the locker room. He, too, planned to swim. Tom greeted
him and introduced himself. The man, in a thick foreign ac-
cent, explained roughly that he is a wrestler by trade and had

come in for a swim, too. Naturally, after their shower and wearing only their shower caps, Tom let his new friend step from the shower room to the pool area first. Thinking Tom would be stepping through the door, Bill let forth a wild yell and jumped on the wrestler's back. Sometime before they hit the water, Bill realized his mistake. Up to the surface came one distressed professor and one wild-eyed wrestler.

The scene was this: one professor was swimming in erratic circles, alternately yelling apologies that were hardly understood and yelling at Tom to help him explain his actions; one wild-eyed wrestler was following one distressed professor in hopes of rearranging the, professor's anatomy; and another professor was standing at the edge of the pool alternately laughing and trying to convince a non-English-speaking wrestler that it was a case of mistaken identity.

Looking back on the incident, Tom said, "I wanted so badly to say of Bill, 'I never saw him before in my life.' "

Thanks! (I Think)

Faculty lounges are notoriously bad places for colleagues to seek sympathy for mundane problems, or to receive affirmation if the colleague seems to be a little pleased with self.

A theology professor strolled into the faculty lounge at noon one day and interrupted conversations with a request: "Can anyone break this five-dollar bill?" "I can," said the archaeology professor. The theology professor handed the five-dollar bill to the archaeology professor who tore it in two, handed the pieces back to the owner, and resumed his conversation.

* * *

An Old Testament professor was notoriously against physical exercise. Frequently, he would quote Bernard Baruch: "I get my exercise being pall bearer for people who exercised."

Just as frequently he would say, "If you ever see me running, look to see what's chasing me."

A preaching professor and an ethics professor made an effort to persuade the Old Testament professor that exercise is good for one's health. Said the preaching professor, "I walk two miles every night and as a result my resting heartbeat is fifty-two beats per minute." Rather than being impressed, the Old Testament professor responded, in mock alarm, "Fifty-two beats a minute. Why, man, your tombstone will say you were dead a long time before you knew it!"

Several months later, the ethics professor, on his first day back on campus after undergoing open heart surgery, determinedly sought the Old Testament professor. He found him in the faculty lounge, marched gingerly over to him and said, "My doctor said that if I had not exercised, I would be dead right now." Undaunted, the Old Testament professor smiled and said, "Now that you have had surgery, you will probably live as long as I do."

Chapter Five

■■■■■

The Witty Humor
of Clever Comebacks

The art of a quick retort is a gift for some people. For a few other people, a quick, witty comeback will occur to them once in a while. For the rest of us, we think of a quick, witty retort anywhere from a few minutes to a few days later. Part of the gift of a quick wit is to be able to strike immediately at the heart of any matter. This quality is a childlike one. The quick-witted person does not allow entanglements in side issues or superficial considerations. Instead, he or she bares the matter immediately and then either describes the situation as it is or contrasts the situation with the way it ought to be. One of the wittiest persons described in this chapter teaches kindergarten. This kindergarten teacher readily testifies that her job keeps her thinking in irreducible terms which, in turn, accounts for much of her ability with a clever comeback.

Notice, in the next three anecdotes, how quickly she reduces three situations to irreducible terms.

The kindergarten teacher saw the preacher at a social gathering. By way of polite conversation, the teacher asked, "How are you?" The preacher thinking it would be clever, answered, "Oh, I'm like Barnabas — I'm a good man full of the Holy Spirit and of faith." "That's not all you're full of," said the teacher.

* * *

It was time for some Friday night fun and fellowship. The three couples decided to treat themselves to a steak dinner. When they arrived at the steak house, they were assigned a number, sent to a crowded, noisy room and told to wait there till their number was called. As they waited, a cocktail waitress came by and said, "Welcome to happy hour, what would you like to drink?" The three couples graciously declined anything from the bar. "Just waiting for a table," they said. Fifteen minutes later, the girl came by again with the same invitation. Again, the couples informed her they were waiting for a table. Five minutes later the girl returned. One of the men had mentioned to the kindergarten teacher that their table was probably being delayed in hopes that they would order something from the bar first. So when the girl came by with her, "Welcome to happy hour" speech again, the kindergarten teacher informed her: "Girl, we are all Baptists and this is as happy as we're going to get, so tell them to get us a table!"

* * *

The preachers in the crowd were talking about the traditional Mother's Day sermons. At one time or another each of them had used Proverbs 31:10-31 as a Mother's Day sermon text. During the conversation, one of the preachers quoted verse 28: "Her children rise up and call her blessed." The kindergarten teacher laughed heartily and said, "I'm half way there. My children call me."

* * *

Forgive the personal reference, but the next anecdote fits the category of reducing the situation to the irreducible. This story first appeared in an "in-house" company newsletter:

Al Fasol habitually answers the telephone: "News room, Al Fasol." One day a woman, apparently angered about some news item she had seen on the six o'clock news, called the station. The conversation went like this:

"News room, Al Fasol."

"Stupid!" shrilled the woman.

"Yes, ma'am, now that we have identified ourselves, how may I help you?" answered Fasol, politely.

Now That You Mention It . . .

The preacher was justifiably proud of his first child, a son. A fellow staff member, with the unfortunate habit of asking personal questions, saw the preacher, his wife, and their son about a month after the child was born. "So, when are you two going to have another baby?" inquired the staff member. "Nine months from tonight," replied the preacher, sarcastically.

* * *

He wore his new mail-order "doctor of theology" degree with inordinate pride, as mail-order "doctors" are prone to do. A woman in his congregation — one of those little old ladies who seem to be commissioned of God to keep upstart preachers humble — looked at him disgustedly and said, "Him a doctor? Why, the only big word he knows is 'mentholatum.' "

* * *

The driver of a large, new car said to the preacher, who was driving a small, eight-year-old car with more than 100,000 miles on it, "The reason I drive a nice car and you do not is I am closer to God than you are." "Yes," answered the preacher, "And what I am thinking about you right now proves you are right."

* * *

The interim pastor drove to the church field every Saturday afternoon and had a sandwich at the same restaurant every Saturday night. The pastor became acquainted with the Saturday supper crowd at that restaurant. On one of those Saturday nights, the usual retinue was there — waitresses, truck drivers, and the interim pastor — when a bright red church bus pulled into the restaurant parking lot. The people on the bus ran to the restaurant, shouting and praying. Groups of four to six surrounded the individual drivers and waitresses. The truck drivers and waitresses were overwhelmed by the people from the bus who were speaking in tongues, asking questions, pointing their fingers, giving dire warnings. The bedlam lasted several minutes before one of the waitresses pointed to the interim pastor, who thus far had been ignored, and said, "Yonder sits a preacher. Why don't you all talk to him?"

The church group, en masse, surrounded the preacher with the same frenzied activity. They shouted warnings at him, such as, "The blood of your congregation is on your hands!" "You are not a true servant of God!" "You don't truly love or believe God!" "Listen to us, Brother, we have the truth, and God have mercy on your soul if you do not receive it from us!"

The interim pastor stood up and moved through the crowd to the cash register. He meant it as a gesture of rejection of the group, and they understood the gesture that way. One of the church group strode up to him and put a finger in his face and yelled, "We are like King David, full of God's love, but you are like King Saul!"

"You have finally said something with which I agree," said the pastor.

"We did?" responded the group, befuddled. "You agree that we are like King David and you are like King Saul?"

"Right," said the pastor. "And you will recall that the first time we meet Saul, he was looking for his father's asses and I have just found them."

* * *

The guest preacher was invited to have dinner at the home of a family which had fourteen children. It was a clean, pleasant, constantly active home. There were more children than there were places to sit. Whenever a family member left a chair, another family member claimed it, unless the person leaving the chair pointed to it and said, "Saved!" Constantly the guest preacher heard someone point to a chair and say, "Saved!" The preacher shared later that there was more salvation in the furniture of that home than he had seen in some churches.

The preacher also participated in the family game. When someone entered the room and saw an empty chair and asked if it were saved, the preacher responded, "No, but it is under conviction."

The Best of Ministers, The Worst of . . .

This will surprise a few naive folks, but there are preachers who work hard to impress the "right" people. Most of these preachers are successful at making an "impression." Sometimes, such preachers wish they had not made the impression they did make. After one lengthy glowing, flattering introduction, one of those "great" preachers sighed and said, "Thank you. I can hardly wait to hear what I have to say."

* * *

There was once a silver-maned, dynamic preacher who loved to burst the balloon of anyone's false pride. This preacher invited a young man to preach a revival at his strong, significant, vibrant church. Until that time the young preacher had been a picture of Christian humility. The invitation to preach a revival at the large, prestigious church changed all of that and the older pastor was visibly perturbed.

During the opening hymn of the first service of the scheduled revival meeting, the older pastor leaned over to the

younger preacher and asked, "What is your text for this sermon?" The young preacher told him the text. "And what is the title of this sermon?" The young preacher told him the title. "And what is your outline for this sermon?" The young preacher shared the outline. "Tell me a little about how you develop that outline. What illustrations will you use?" The young preacher, a little distraught now, told him how the sermon would be developed and illustrated.

Later in the service, the older pastor introduced the young preacher. During the introduction, the older preacher said, "I remember a sermon this man preached once . . ." and he proceeded to share the text, title, outline, and illustrations of the sermon that the young preacher had just shared. "After our special music, we will hear what this young preacher has to share with us today," said the older preacher as he walked off of the platform, leaving a younger preacher frantically looking for another text, title, outline . . .

* * *

Startled to hear one of his sermons during a morning worship service, the older preacher was restless. At the close of the service, he asked the pastor how long it took him to prepare that sermon.

"The better part of a day," replied the pastor.

"Congratulations," said the older preacher. "It took me sixty-three years."

* * *

The speaker was impressed with himself. Perhaps, he had reason to be; nevertheless he was. He mentioned that he used to do his presentations on radio, but decided that it would be much more considerate of himself to do his speaking on television. "That way," he stated seriously, "people can see me as well as hear me." And so the congregation received an overdose of the gospel according the "I," "me," and "my." The speaker did have humility, but he took pride in that, too.

When his arrogant self-promoting was finally concluded, and he strutted to his seat, someone in the gallery shouted, "There but for the grace of God, goes God!"

* * *

The pastor bragged that he had baptized some people as often as ". . . five, six, seven times each." "That is why," retorted another pastor, "your baptistry is known as the Robo Car Wash!"

* * *

The pastor was "numbers"-conscious. It occurred to the pastor that it would be wonderful to report that ten thousand persons attended Sunday church school on Easter day. The pastor called a staff meeting to share his vision with them. "But that's twice our weekly average," a staff member protested. "No problem," answered the pastor, "I will make available all the funding you will need to promote a ten-thousand-in-Sunday-school attendance day. I know you can do it and you know you had better do it." The pastor left the staff to formulate their plans.

The following Easter, slightly more than ten thousand persons were reported as in attendance for Sunday school. Someone complimented the staff by saying, "So, you pulled it off. Good for you." "Good for us," replied a staff member, "unless some fool actually makes an accurate count."

* * *

The kindly man who led the benediction was just "telling it like it is" when he prayed, "Lord, we don't understand what was said this morning. I pray you will help us apply it to our lives anyway. Amen."

That prayer is reminiscent of the person who wrote: "Preachers are persons who tell you many things you never knew before and about which you will not be certain afterwards."

A similar but much more colorful prayer was offered by a lady who said, "Lord, Lord, when our brother preaches, help him deliver those groceries to a lower shelf."

* * *

The elderly lady called the pastor's home at 12:30 a.m. three to five nights a week. Invariably, after the pastor's sleepy "Hello," the lady would say, "Pastor, you're not in bed already are you?" She then would berate him for not watching a late night talk show: "There is vulgarity and profanity on that show, and you're asleep while the devil works. We must do something to get that show off the air, and I expect to be able to discuss such matters with my pastor!"

The pastor was in the habit of rising around 5:30 each morning for devotional time and study. He realized that this past-midnight telephone intrusion was taxing to his inherent good nature. The lady, however, insisted and persisted on calling at 12:30 a.m. and saying, "Pastor, you're not in bed already are you?"

Finally, he saw the obvious solution to his dilemma. At 5:30 a.m. he called her. In response to *her* sleepy "Hello," he said, "You're not still in bed are you? Now, about that matter you wanted to discuss a few hours ago . . ."

* * *

The young wife had just been converted to Christianity.

Every church has a self-appointed church theologian. This church's self-appointed church theologian came to visit the new convert to share the pop-theology of the moment, which was: the wife must reverence the husband, no matter what.

The new convert shifted uncomfortably and said, "But he doesn't believe in church or go to church. He's sitting right here, why don't you talk to him?"

The self-appointed church theologian pursed his lips and smiled a "V"-shaped smile that is reserved only for self-appointed church theologians, "Nevertheless, it is the accepted biblical stance that you reverence your husband. Do you want to live by the Bible or not?"

The new convert surely wanted to live by the Bible, but not without integrity, so she looked at her husband and said, "You're a big, fat slob, and I guess you're my Lord and Master, so tell me what you want me to do."

* * *

Even in her later years, friends would ask the English teacher, "You are so attractive. Why have you never married?" The teacher learned to suppress asking, "Why is attractiveness the main qualification for marriage?" However, she did learn how to answer the question. The conversation went like this:

"You're so attractive. Why have you never married?"

"I've never married because of what the Bible says."

Pause. "Oh, you mean 1 Corinthians 7 where Paul says it is better not to marry?"

"No, I do not mean 1 Corinthians 7. I do mean 1 Thessalonians 4:13."

Longer pause. "Isn't that where Paul talks about the dead in Christ rising first? That doesn't have anything to do with marriage!"

"Sure it does! Read verse 13 carefully and you will see why I never married. Verse 13 clearly says, 'I would not have you ignorant brethren' and that is why I never married."

* * *

The army general and a priest did not like one another. They had known each other for years, and the dislike had increased when the priest was assigned as a chaplain to the general's base. The priest had become obese. The general was military slim. They did not like each other when they were passengers on the same plane returning for a high school reunion. When they "accidentally" bumped into each other in a buffet line, the priest said, "Pardon me, Conductor." To which the general responded, "A woman in your condition shouldn't be here."

A Word in Time Saves . . .

The enactment of the Lord's Supper was impressive. The costumes were authentic looking. The cast handled their roles well, until the actor portraying the Lord forgot to say to the actor portraying Judas, "That thou doest, do quickly." (John 13:27) Judas waited. The cast waited. The congregation waited. The actor portraying the Lord seemed unaware that he had omitted an important line. Eventually, "Judas" tapped "the Lord" on the shoulder and said, "Excuse me, Lord, could we talk?"

An Element of Surprise

The colonel constantly picked at the chaplain. The prayers lack force, the sermons lack power, the services are a drag. The chaplain listened and tried to improve. Trying to improve seemed to increase the colonel's criticisms. "Specifically, what do you want me to do?" complained the chaplain. "Surprise me," responded the colonel.

Boy, was the colonel surprised when he came to the altar

to receive a wafer. The chaplain gave him an oatmeal cookie, instead.

* * *

The hispanic preacher reached into his pocket and pulled out a small bag containing tiny pellets. The hispanic preacher sprinkled several of the pellets over his food. "What is that?" asked the host. "Seasoning," answered the preacher. "May I have some?" asked the host. "Certainly," replied the preacher.

The pellets were made of hot pepper. The host ate some. The host gagged, choked, broke into a sweat, and wiped away tears. "Too hot?" inquired the preacher. The host gasped, "I've heard hell-fire sermons before, but you are the first preacher I've known who carries samples around with him!"

Knowing When to Quit

In the spirit of the biblical record of the wedding feast at Cana (John 2), this story is saved for the last.

When he was called to pastor his first church, he had been a Christian for just two years. During that time he had worked a Sunday-through-Friday schedule at a small radio station. Thus, his first two years as a Christian he spent his Sundays either at a radio station or as a supply preacher. Consequently, there was a lot about church and church people that he had not experienced.

Some of this naivete must have been obvious. Soon after accepting the call, one of the elderly gentlemen of the church drew him aside and said, "Let me tell you about everyone else in this church." The new pastor didn't know at the time that there is a person in every church who delights in telling "about everyone else in this church." The gentleman concluded his little tirade with some advice: "You will want to avoid Mrs. _____. She is very frank and forthright and you don't have enough experience to get along with her."

The new pastor was prepared to heed his advice. But something deep inside kept asking, "What is so bad about a person who speaks frankly and forthrightly?" Eventually, the pastor decided to make Mr. and Mrs. _____'s home the target of his first pastoral visit. The pastor drove around the block several times, hoping they would leave so he could knock on the door and later report to the church: "I tried to visit the _____ family today, but they weren't home." But they didn't leave and the pastor worked up the courage to knock on the front door. They had a screen door that was difficult for those on the outside to see through. In what the pastor described as a female, top sergeant voice, someone said, "Yes?"

The pastor asked, "Mrs. _____?"

He was relieved when the female top sergeant voice said, "No."

So the pastor graciously replied, "Please tell Mrs. _____ that her new pastor came by to see her today," and with a feeling of relief he started toward his car.

The female, top sergeant voice had a quality that made you feel you better do whatever it said. This female, top sergeant voice then said, "Young preacher! You get yourself back here!" So he did.

When she opened the door to let him in he was confused. Now that he could see her, he realized she was Mrs. _____ and she just said she wasn't. She chuckled at his discomfort and said, "You're young enough to be my grandson and my grandchildren call me 'Mammaw.' So don't call me Mrs. _____, call me Mammaw." So he did.

That afternoon was a beautiful experience. The _____s were salt-of-the-earth people and they loved each other immediately. Mr. _____ was quiet but enjoyed life immensely. Mammaw had one of the fastest, sharpest minds the pastor had ever met. She didn't have an opportunity for formal education, but that did not deter her mental growth. She knew quickly that the pastor couldn't match her mental quickness and dedicated herself from then on to teasing him almost mercilessly. What a contrast they were. He was working his way through college, yet he never had the last word in their frequent exchanges.

In 1963 the pastor left the church to attend seminary. The pastor's mother had not been in good health. For that and other reasons he went back for visits at home during Christmas vacations. The folks at his first pastorate always enjoyed fellowship and always arranged a get-together while he was visiting his parents who lived near the church.

Mammaw was really being kind at the 1963 gathering when she asked, "Brother, tell us what you learned at seminary this year." The question caught him off guard. He started to parse a Greek verb but decided she wouldn't be interested in that. He couldn't think of a theological gem at the moment and the result was that he stammered and hesitated. Mammaw, of course, caught on quickly and gleefully shouted, "Sounds to me like you better go back for another year!"

Mammaw probably could hardly wait for next Christmas. So in 1964, while he was relaxing at another Christmas fellowship in the same church, Mammaw waited till the crowd was at its peak and inquired, "Brother, did you learn anything at all in seminary this year?" He was caught off guard again. He started to analyze the Nicene Creed, or the JEPD theory, or to tell her about Balthasar Hubmaier. But none of that seemed appropriate. The result was the same. He stammered and hesitated and Mammaw said, "I think you better go back for another year!"

However, that night made him decide to be prepared for next Christmas. He wanted, just once, to have the last word with Mammaw. He committed himself to thorough preparation. On January 2, 1965, during the long drive back to seminary, he plotted a way to get ahead of Mammaw just once. Mammaw was nearly eighty years old and he was working on a Master's degree and yet she could dissect him at will with that incisive mind of hers.

He was on I-30 between Little Rock and Benton,

Arkansas, when his "vision" came. The next time he saw Mammaw, he decided, he would pull an old preacher's joke. He would walk up to Mammaw and say "The Bible says there won't be any women in heaven!" And then he would quote Revelation 8:1 "and when the seventh seal was opened, there was a silence in heaven for about the space of an half an hour."

It was a long year for the former pastor. Would he get home at Christmas? Would the church have another Christmas fellowship? Would Mammaw come if they did? Would she ask her question one more time? The answer to all the questions was yes. He could tell by the twinkle in her eyes that she was going to ask the question again. Sure enough she did. Oh, he was so glad she asked! He had waited for this moment. He walked to the center of the room to better enjoy the moment. Conversations stopped. Everyone gazed at him sympathetically. With a ring of confidence in his voice — the kind of sound preachers have when they are pompous — he said, "Yes, Mammaw, I learned something in seminary this year. (Dramatic pause) I learned that the Bible says there won't be any women in heaven."

But as soon as he had the words out of his mouth and certainly before he could quote Revelation 8:1, Mammaw retorted: "I'll tell you one thing — the men won't stay!"

Later, feeling a bit penitent, Mammaw encouraged the young preacher to finish his joke. The preacher resisted. He explained, "I didn't know what she would say after I quoted the Scripture!"

There was, as you would expect, more to this relationship than just teasing. Whenever that young preacher called Mammaw, or saw her in church or anywhere, Mammaw's first words always were: "I pray for you every day!" Behind each of the anecdotes shared in this book there are similar relationships. Truly, no one has as much fun and joy in life than do Christians. Christian joy plumbs the depths of a person's soul. Christian fun reveals the worst in us and brings out the best in us. Laughing together brings a bonding together that is as deep as crying together. There have been many worth-while books written of the trials and burdens of Christianity. It seemed to be time for a glimpse of the *fun* of Christianity.

About the Author

The world of communication has fascinated Al Fasol since 1953. While a junior in high school, Fasol enrolled in a speech class. The teacher, frustrated with Fasol's dry humor, punished him one day by demanding that he sing the front page of a newspaper before the class. Somehow, during that experience, Fasol realized that a speaker can control the audience simply by a vocal inflection, or a gesture, or a facial expression.

This fascination first led Fasol to a major in speech at Southern Illinois University and then to a career in broadcasting. Fasol became a Christian at age twenty-one and soon felt that his gifts and training in public speaking were to be used in the ministry. His broadcasting career ended at WBAP in Fort Worth, Texas, where he did both radio and television newscasting. His pastoral career included the First Baptist Churches of Royalton, Illinois; Powderly, Texas; and Pennington, Texas. Fasol joined the faculty of Southwestern Baptist Theological Seminary in Fort Worth, Texas, in 1973.

Fasol and his wife Beverly were married in 1960. They have three children: Robert, Vivian, and Malinda. Beverly has a degree from Southwestern Seminary and is working on a degree at Dallas Baptist University. Robert holds a Bachelor's and Master's degree in music from Texas Christian University. Vivian has Bachelor's degree in Speech Pathology from Hardin Simons University and plans to work on advanced degrees in the same field. Malinda plans to major in physical therapy in college.

Life began for Al Fasol on June 6, 1937, in Chicago, Illinois. He and his family moved to West Frankfort, Illinois, in 1950. Fasol moved from West Frankfort after finishing high school there in 1955. The move from a major metropolis to a small town, he often says, was roughly comparable to moving from Earth to Mars. "There was little about city life that related to small-town life," Fasol says. "However, there was a world of opportunity available to me in the excellent school system in West Frankfort that was not available to me in inner-city Chicago."